The Story of Us: Becoming Human

Written by Michael Haralambos and Wendy Hope

CW00550854

Contents

Collins

Introduction

This book looks at human evolution – how we changed from ape-like beings to the humans we are today.

Look at this picture of today's humans. We all seem very different. Our skin has different shades and tones; our hair is red, blonde, black or brown. But these differences are very small. We are all humans – we are all part of the same human family.

humans today

The next picture is an artist's view of how we might have looked millions of years ago. Our **ancestors** then were much shorter than we are today, and their brains were four times smaller than ours. These are important differences between our ancient relatives and ourselves.

What is evolution?

All living things evolve – they gradually change into something new. This change can take millions of years. This book looks at human evolution. It looks at where we came from and how we became today's human beings.

The story of human evolution is not a straight line. At any one time, there were different types of human-like beings. Sometimes these different types met, mixed and had children together. This mixing is part of human evolution.

The scientific name for today's humans is *Homo sapiens* (sap-ee-ens) which means "wise human". We first evolved as *Homo sapiens* over 300 thousand years ago.

A lot of what we know about human evolution has been learnt from **fossils**. Fossils are the remains of once-living creatures that have turned to stone after thousands of years. Usually fossils are the hard parts of a creature such as teeth and bone, as the soft parts such as skin and muscle rot away quickly. Fossils can give us an idea about what our ancestors were like, for example how tall they were, how long their arms were and how big their brains were.

1 In the beginning

Our story begins when we started to change from our ape-like ancestors and become more like the humans we are today. It begins when apes spent less time in the trees and more time on the ground, and when they started to stand upright and walk on two legs. We think this happened between seven and five million years ago in Africa.

Although apes can stand upright, they usually walk on all fours as shown in this picture of chimpanzees. This type of walking is called knuckle-walking.

chimpanzees walking on all fours

The first hominins (hom-in-ins)

Our early ancestors probably lived in the forests all over Africa, but their fossilised bones have only been found in a few places such as Chad, Kenya and Ethiopia. Like us, they are called **hominins**. A hominin has one or more features which are like human features but which are not found in apes such as chimpanzees. The earliest hominins have both human-like and ape-like features.

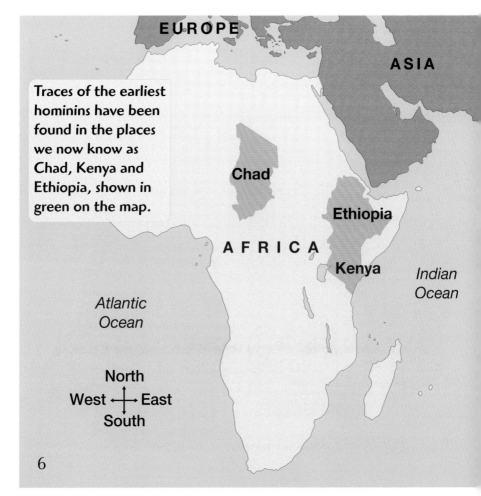

Traces of the earliest hominins have been found in the places we now know as Chad, Kenya and Ethiopia, shown in green on the map.

EUROPE

ASIA

Chad

Ethiopia

AFRICA

Kenya

Atlantic Ocean

Indian Ocean

North

West ←┼→ East

South

Fossils from the earliest hominins indicate that they walked on two legs in an upright position. This is a human-like feature. The fossils also show that they had some ape-like features: long, strong arms and powerful upper bodies which were good for climbing trees. They probably lived in the trees and on the ground. They could find plenty of food in both places. In this book, we have chosen to focus on two examples of these early hominins.

Sahelanthropus (say-hel-an-throw-pus)

The earliest hominin we know about is called *Sahelanthropus*. Its fossil skull was found in Chad in central Africa where it lived about seven million years ago.

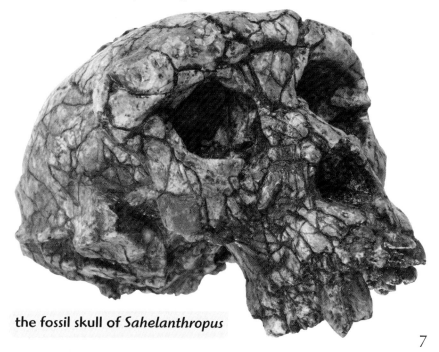

the fossil skull of *Sahelanthropus*

In some ways, *Sahelanthropus* was ape-like. It had a small ape-like brain about the size of a chimpanzee's. It also had large brow ridges, the bones that go over the eyes. This can be seen in the artist's picture below.

an artist's view of *Sahelanthropus*

In some ways, *Sahelanthropus* was human-like. This can be seen from the opening underneath its skull where the backbone joins. The opening is near the middle of the skull which allows the head to balance in an upright position for walking on two legs. For apes, such as chimpanzees, the opening is nearer the back of the skull which indicates that they are less upright than humans and walk on all fours.

This difference is shown in the pictures below. Notice the underside of the skull and the hole where the backbone goes into the skull.

chimpanzee   Homo sapiens   Sahelanthropus

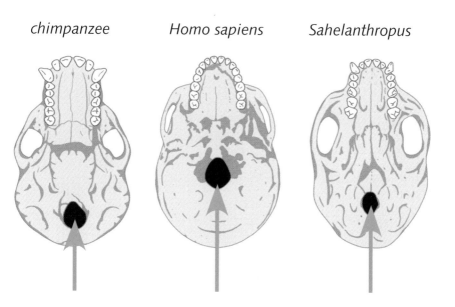

This mixture of human-like and ape-like features was found in the early hominins.

Ardipithecus (ar-dee-pith-icus)

The next hominin we know about is called *Ardipithecus*, which means "ground ape". Fossils of more than 40 of these hominins have been found in Ethiopia in East Africa where they lived from about 5.8 to 4.5 million years ago. The fossils were usually very small – teeth and bits of bones. A female skeleton of over 100 parts was pieced together. Scientists called her Ardi.

Ardi probably weighed about 50 kg and was about 120 cms tall. She had a small brain about the size of a chimpanzee's. Her hip and leg bones showed she could walk on two legs. Her long arms and long, curved fingers helped her to climb trees.

Ardi's fossil skull

The plant fossils found nearby showed that Ardi lived in forests of fig and palm trees. She may have eaten nuts, fruit, leaves, roots and insects.

Ardi was a "ground ape": she could walk on the ground as well as climb in trees.

2 *Australopithecus* (ostra-low-pith-icus)

Australopithecus is the name given to some groups of hominins who lived in Africa from about 4.2 million to 1.9 million years ago. *Australopithecus* means "southern ape".

In 2016, the oldest known *Australopithecus* skull was found in Ethiopia in Africa. It was about 3.8 million years old and belonged to a type of *Australopithecus* called *Australopithecus anamensis*. The left-hand picture below shows the skull. It was probably an adult male. The picture on the right is an artist's view of what *Australopithecus anamensis* may have looked like.

The skull shows he had a small brain, about a quarter of the size of our human brain. Other fossil bones of *Australopithecus anamensis* show he probably walked on two legs. Like *Sahelanthropus* and *Ardipithecus*, he had a mixture of human-like and ape-like features.

Australopithecus anamensis

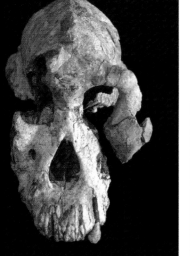
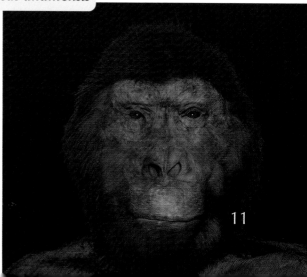

Finding Lucy – *Australopithicus afarensis* (af-ar-en-sis)

It was November 1974. It had been a long, hot day in Ethiopia, a country in Africa. A group of scientists were looking for fossil bones. They were hoping to find the bones of our early ancestors.

Two of the scientists spotted a fossil bone sticking out of the ground. It looked like a human elbow bone. Nearby they found a fossil thigh bone, part of a skull, some ribs and a lower jaw.

Back at camp, they showed their finds to the rest of the group. Everybody was very excited. Could these be the bones of one of our very early relatives? That evening they celebrated their find round the campfire, playing their favourite song *Lucy in the Sky with Diamonds.* Later they found out that the bones belonged to a female and decided to call her Lucy.

During the next two weeks, the team found many more of Lucy's bones. The bones were about 3.2 million years old. Using them as a guide, artists have drawn pictures to give an idea of what Lucy might have looked like.

Lucy's fossilised bones – Although fully grown, she was only the height of a five year old today.

an artist's view of Lucy

13

Lucy was a hominin. Her skeleton was a bit like an ape's and a bit like a human's. Her arms and fingers were much longer than those of recent humans. Her arm bones were thick and strong, and she had a powerful upper body. This was good for climbing trees.

Other parts of Lucy's skeleton were more human-like. The shape of her hips, legs and feet bones show that she could stand upright and walk on two legs.

Life on the ground – *Australopithecus* walking upright on two legs.

We can tell from Lucy's skeleton that part of her life was probably spent in trees and part of her life on the ground. She lived in a mixture of woodland, grassland and river valleys, with trees and bushes providing food such as nuts, fruit, berries, grasses and leaves.

Lucy was a type of *Australopithecus* called *Australopithecus afarensis*. *Australopithecus* are probably one of our early ancestors.

Life in the trees – *Australopithecus* climbing trees to gather fruit.

15

The picture below shows some of the earliest stone tools made by hominins. They were found in Kenya and are about 3.3 million years old. They may have been made by *Australopithecus*. Some of these tools are sharp flakes struck from larger stones. They were probably used for cutting.

some of the earliest stone tools made by hominins

Fossils are not the only evidence we use to learn about human evolution, as the following pictures show.

These footprints were made in ash from a volcano about 3.7 million years ago. Fossil teeth and jaws were found nearby and they are like Lucy's. The footprints look like they were made by *Australopithecus* walking on two legs.

Years later, another set of footprints was found in the same volcanic ash. They were probably made by five *Australopithecus* including a child who left a trail of smaller footprints in the ash. An artist's view of the five is shown below.

footprints in Tanzania

This is a timeline from seven million years ago until today.
It shows how long we think *Sahelanthropus*, *Ardipithecus* and
Australopithecus lived in Africa.

Timeline

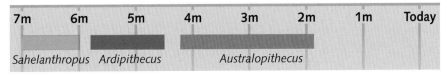

The timelines in this book only show the hominins we think are
most important for human evolution. There are many other
types of hominins.

The dates for the timelines and the hominins are based on
the dates of fossils.

Australopithecus: **in brief**

The early hominins had both human and
ape-like features. Their fossil bones show
they could stand upright and walk on two legs.
They probably lived in the trees and on the ground.
Some of the earliest stone tools made by hominins
were made by *Australopithecus*.

3 *Homo habilis* (hab-i-lis) – handy human

Around 2.4 million years ago, a new type of hominin evolved in Africa. Scientists called them *Homo habilis*, which means "handy humans". *Homo* means "human". They were called this because they were more like today's humans than earlier hominins. They were called *habilis*, meaning "skilful", because the stone tools they made showed skill and expertise.

Homo habilis probably evolved from *Australopithecus*. However, there is not a clear and direct line from one to the other. There were a number of different hominins living in Africa at the time. Some of them may have had children together and some of these children may have evolved into *Homo habilis*.

Homo habilis fossils and the tools they made have been found in places such as Ethiopia, Kenya, Tanzania and South Africa.

map of Africa showing these places in green

Body and brain

Homo habilis looked much the same as *Australopithecus*. They were about the same body shape and size, weight and height. Their bones showed they stood upright and walked on two legs.

The main difference was that *Homo habilis* had a larger brain. It was about 50% larger than an *Australopithecus* brain.

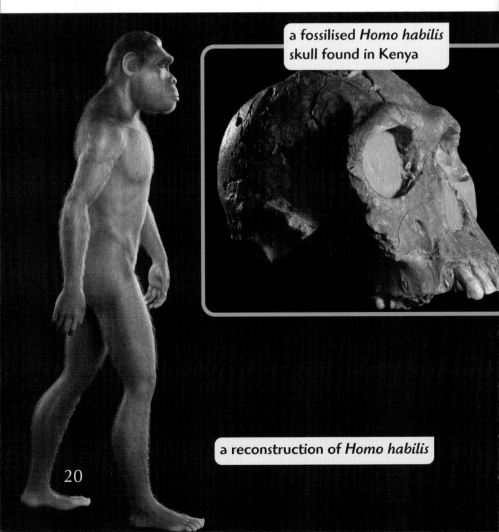

a fossilised *Homo habilis* skull found in Kenya

a reconstruction of *Homo habilis*

an artist's view of a female *Homo habilis*

Making stone tools

Thousands of stone tools have been found near the fossil bones of *Homo habilis*. The tools were made with stones which were hit against other stones to strike off sharp flakes. Two main types of tools were made: choppers and flake tools.

Homo habilis striking a stone to remove a sharp flake

chopper tool found near *Homo habilis* bones in Tanzania

Cut marks have been found on animal bones alongside *Homo habilis* fossils. Chopper tools were probably used for cutting up an animal and smashing bones to eat the marrow inside. Sharp flake tools were probably used for skinning animals and cutting meat from the bones.

It was once thought that *Homo habilis* were the first tool makers. Since then, however, stone tools and animal bones with cut marks have been found that are over half a million years older than *Homo habilis*. *Australopithecus* were making stone tools and eating meat before *Homo habilis* evolved.

drawing of a flake tool found near *Homo habilis* bones in Tanzania

***Homo habilis* cutting up and skinning an antelope using a chopper and a flake tool**

23

Climate and food

During the time of *Homo habilis* (2.4 to 1.6 million years ago), there was a big change in the climate in parts of Africa. Over a long time, it became cooler and drier. Grassland expanded and there were fewer forested areas. There were more grass-eating animals such as antelopes and zebras.

The higher number of grass-eating animals may have led to changes in the food eaten by *Homo habilis*. They may have spent more time hunting and scavenging (getting meat from the kills made by other animals or from animals that had just died).

antelope on grassland called savannah

Compared to many plant foods, meat provided more energy and was digested more easily. We don't think *Homo habilis* were able to cook meat – they probably just ate it raw. Fruit, nuts, berries, leaves and grasses were probably still their main food.

Homo habilis: **in brief**

Homo habilis looked similar to *Australopithecus*. The main difference was that *Homo habilis* had a larger brain. Some of their features, such as their teeth and jaw, were more human-like.

Homo habilis were skilful tool makers. They probably spent more time hunting than *Australopithecus* and ate more meat. We think their main food was still fruit, nuts, berries, leaves and grasses.

Timeline

7m	6m	5m	4m	3m	2m	1m	Today

Sahelanthropus   *Ardipithecus*   *Australopithecus*

Homo habilis

4 *Homo erectus* (e-rec-tus) – upright human

Homo erectus, which means "upright human", started life in Africa about 2 million years ago and died out about 100 thousand years ago.

Compared with *Homo habilis*, *Homo erectus* had longer legs and a larger brain: they were taller, heavier and probably cleverer, and better at walking and running.

Some of these differences can be seen from the picture below.

Homo habilis

Homo erectus

From the clues that fossil bones give us, artists have drawn pictures of what *Homo habilis* and *Homo erectus* probably looked like. *Homo erectus* looked more like us than *Homo habilis* did. But there were still important differences between *Homo erectus* and *Homo sapiens*. *Homo erectus* had smaller brains than us, a lower forehead, bigger brow ridges over the eyes and very little chin.

Some of these differences can be seen in the pictures below.

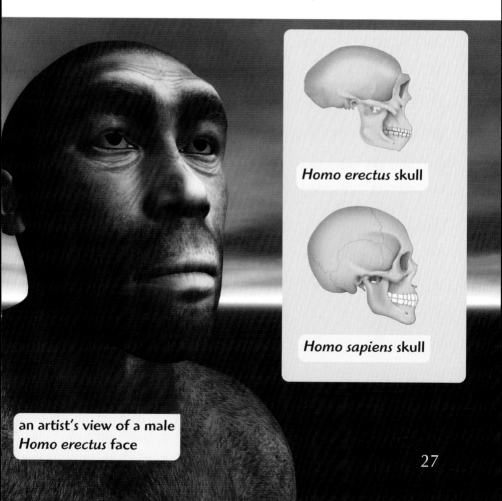

Homo erectus **skull**

Homo sapiens **skull**

an artist's view of a male *Homo erectus* face

Leaving Africa

We think that *Homo erectus* was the first hominin to leave Africa, about 1.8 million years ago. In Africa, *Homo erectus* fossils have been found in Ethiopia, Kenya, Tanzania, South Africa, Algeria and Morocco. *Homo erectus* fossils have also been found in Georgia, China and Indonesia. Bones which may have belonged to *Homo erectus* have been found in Spain and Italy.

The last-known *Homo erectus* fossils were found on Java, an island in Indonesia. These were dated to around 100 thousand years ago.

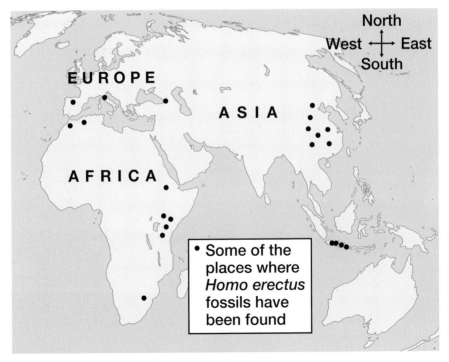

• Some of the places where *Homo erectus* fossils have been found

Stone tools

The earliest stone tools made by *Homo erectus* were like those made by *Homo habilis*. Around 1.7 million years ago, *Homo erectus* in Africa began to make axes to be held in the hand. Hand axes became the main tool used by hominins for well over a million years.

The pictures show the side and the edge of two hand axes made from flint. A hand axe is not easy to make and needs a lot of skill. A block of flint is hit on one side with a stone. This removes a flake from the other side. This is repeated many times on each side. Sometimes a bone or a horn was also used as a hammer.

Hand axes were probably used for all sorts of things – cutting up animals, skinning them, taking meat off the bone, digging up roots to eat and cutting wood.

hand axes with sharp edges and flakes removed from both sides

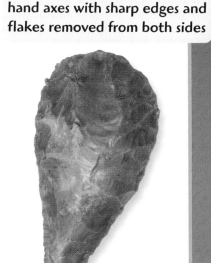

29

Hunting and cooking

We think *Homo erectus* spent more time hunting and ate more meat than *Homo habilis*. Meat is a high-energy food. If it is cooked, it gives much more energy than if it is eaten raw.

In some places, burnt animal bones have been found alongside *Homo erectus* bones. This could mean that meat had been cooked before it was eaten. We don't know if *Homo erectus* started their own fires or if they used wildfires – fires which had started in nature.

Homo erectus cooking meat over a campfire

Looking for evidence of *Homo erectus*

These footprints were found in what used to be a muddy lakeside in Kenya, Africa. Ninety-nine footprints were found all going in the same direction, dated from 1.5 million years ago. They may have been left by a small hunting group of *Homo erectus*. Alongside were the footprints of antelopes, wildebeest, gazelles and hippos.

In eastern China, a skull and teeth of *Homo erectus* were found with stone tools and over six thousand bones from animals such as giant elephants and giant pandas.

footprints in Kenya probably made by *Homo erectus*

Homo erectus: **in brief**

Homo erectus was a lot more like us than *Homo habilis*. But there were still important differences such as brain size between *Homo erectus* and ourselves.

Homo erectus made hand axes, the main multi-purpose tool used by hominins for over a million years. We think they spent more time hunting and ate more meat than *Homo habilis* and sometimes they may have cooked the meat.

Timeline

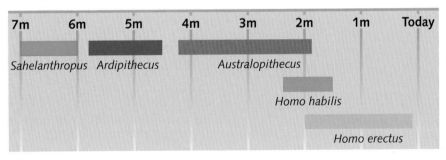

5 Homo heidelbergensis
(hi-del-burg-ensis)

We are now getting closer to *Homo sapiens* – to being us.

Homo heidelbergensis had a mixture of *Homo erectus* and *Homo sapiens* features. Their name came from a fossil jawbone found near Heidelberg in Germany. They probably evolved from *Homo erectus*.

The oldest known *Homo heidelbergensis* fossil is about 640 thousand years old. The most recent is around 200 thousand years old. Their bones and tools have been found in places such as Morocco, Ethiopia, Zambia, South Africa, England, France, Germany, Portugal, Italy, Hungary and Greece, as shown on the map.

Homo heidelbergensis probably moved from place to place because of changes in climate, vegetation, animal life and the need for more food and space.

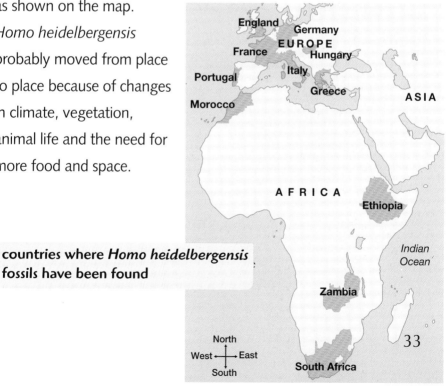

countries where *Homo heidelbergensis* fossils have been found

33

Boxgrove – amazing discoveries

We can learn a lot about *Homo heidelbergensis* from **excavations** near Boxgrove, a village in the south of England. Stone tools had been found in the area. This led scientists to look further. They made some exciting finds.

excavations at Boxgrove

A hand axe from Boxgrove. Hand axes were the main tools used by *Homo heidelbergensis*.

Over 400 flint hand axes were dug up. The fossilised bones of large animals – rhinoceroses, elephants, horses, bison and red deer – were also found. Many of them had been cut up for eating. The bones had cut marks made from sharp hand axes. The flint to make hand axes had been dug out of the nearby chalk cliffs. Some of the earliest known bone tools in Europe were also found at Boxgrove.

What makes scientists think that *Homo heidelbergensis* lived at Boxgrove? First, because two teeth and a shin bone (the bone below the knee) were found there. They are like the bones of *Homo heidelbergensis* found in other places. Second, because the stone tools from Boxgrove are similar to those found with *Homo heidelbergensis* bones in both Europe and Africa.

Bones

We can learn a lot about *Homo heidelbergensis* from their bones. From their skulls, we find that their brain is only a little smaller than our modern human brain. *Homo heidelbergensis* had thick bones, which indicates powerful muscles. Their forehead sloped back, they had little or no chin and the brow ridges over their eyes were heavy. They were about as tall as us.

an artist's view of *Homo heidelbergensis* based on their skulls

front and side view of a skull found in Africa

Hunting

As the Boxgrove excavations show, *Homo heidelbergensis* were hunters. They probably used spears. The shoulder bone of a horse found at Boxgrove had a hole which may have been made by a spear. Sometimes the spears were wooden poles sharpened at one end. Wooden spears dating from around 320 thousand years ago have been found in Germany, along with the bones of several horses. These wooden spears are known as thrusting spears because they were held and thrust or jabbed into the animals.

From about 500 thousand years ago, *Homo heidelbergensis* also used stone-tipped spears. Stone tips have been found in South Africa. Stone-tipped spears can be thrown for about ten to 30 metres so animals can be killed from a distance. These kind of spears are less dangerous for the hunter to use and more likely to kill than wooden spears.

This 320-thousand-year-old spear tip made of wood was found in south-east England.

***Homo heidelbergensis* stone spear points**

The picture opposite shows *Homo heidelbergensis* skinning and cutting up a rhinoceros. Large animals were probably hunted by a group of people as they could be dangerous and hard to kill.

Homo heidelbergensis: **in brief**

Homo heidelbergensis had both *Homo erectus* and *Homo sapiens* features. Their brain was only a little smaller than that of *Homo sapiens*. Their thick bones indicate they had powerful muscles. *Homo heidelbergensis* hunted large animals using wooden spears and stone-tipped spears.

Timeline

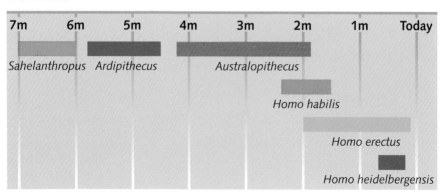

| 7m | 6m | 5m | 4m | 3m | 2m | 1m | Today |

Sahelanthropus *Ardipithecus*

Australopithecus

Homo habilis

Homo erectus

Homo heidelbergensis

37

6 *Homo neanderthalensis* – Neanderthals (nee-an-der-tals)

Around 430 thousand years ago, a new hominin called *Homo neanderthalensis* was present in Europe. They later became widespread in Europe and Asia. The name means "human from the Neander Valley", which is a valley in Germany where Neanderthal fossils were found. Most scientists think that Neanderthals evolved from *Homo heidelbergensis*.

The dark orange section of the map shows where Neanderthals probably lived – between Wales and Portugal in the west and Siberia in the east. During cold periods, sea levels were lower and England was joined to Europe, so Neanderthals could reach England and Wales by walking.

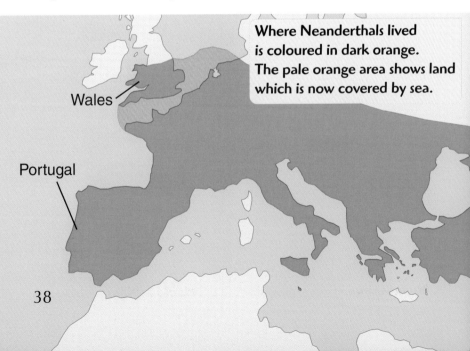

Where Neanderthals lived is coloured in dark orange. The pale orange area shows land which is now covered by sea.

Wales

Portugal

For part of the time, Neanderthals lived in cold areas. Scientists think that the cold, icy weather helped to shape their bodies. Neanderthals were stocky and well-built with wide shoulders, strong arms and powerful chest muscles. They could probably move more quickly than us and having rounder bodies meant they lost less body heat.

Being fast and powerful gave them the speed and strength to hunt big animals such as woolly mammoths, bison and reindeer. The picture shows some of the similarities and differences between Neanderthal and *Homo sapiens*.

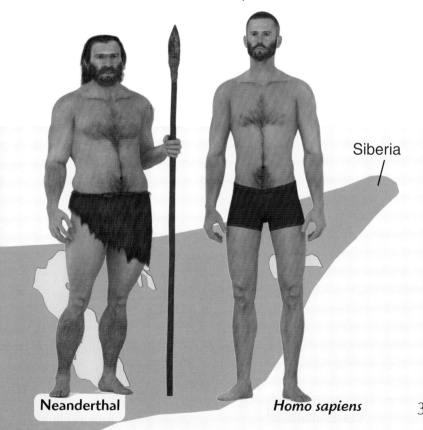

Siberia

Neanderthal

Homo sapiens

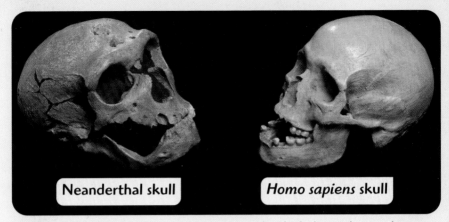

Neanderthal skull

Homo sapiens **skull**

Compared with *Homo sapiens*, Neanderthals have larger brow ridges – the bones above the eyes. They have little or no chin. Their foreheads at the front of the skull slope backwards, while the back of their skull is longer than ours.

Neanderthals' brains are about the same size as *Homo sapiens'* brains. But size isn't everything. Our skull has a higher, more upright forehead. This contains the front part of the brain where we think and plan. The back part of Neanderthal's brain is larger than ours. This part deals with sight, movement and control of the body.

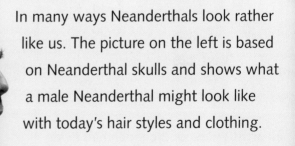

In many ways Neanderthals look rather like us. The picture on the left is based on Neanderthal skulls and shows what a male Neanderthal might look like with today's hair styles and clothing.

No Neanderthal clothes have been found and neither have the type of bone needles which were used by later hominins to make clothes. But they must have worn skins when the weather was extremely cold.

an artist's view of Neanderthals living in a cold area

Hunting, food and fire

Animal bones found in the caves where Neanderthals often lived show that they ate large amounts of meat. The bones also show that they hunted larger animals. Bones of woolly mammoths, bison and reindeer have been found in caves in the colder areas of northern Europe.

Neanderthals living in warmer areas often hunted smaller animals like wild sheep, goats, cattle, horses and red deer.

On sea coasts such as Gibraltar, Neanderthals ate cockles, mussels, limpets, crabs and seals. Neanderthals also ate plant food like vegetables, nuts, roots, fruit and berries. We know this because starch from plants has been found on their fossilised teeth and the remains of nuts, berries and roots in their fossilised waste.

woolly mammoths

Meat is a rich food giving high amounts of energy. Neanderthals needed this to support their muscular bodies and for a life spent hunting, often in very cold weather. Cooking meat makes it easier and quicker to digest. Scientists have found burnt animal bones and stone fireplaces which show that Neanderthals cooked meat over open fires. Apart from cooking, fires gave warmth, light and scared away wild animals.

Did Neanderthals know how to start fires? The marks on their flint hand axes show that they probably did. Some of the Neanderthal hand axes show marks which may have been made by striking them with **pyrite** stone to make sparks.

an artist's model of Neanderthals hunting a woolly mammoth

Life was hard for Neanderthals. Not many lived to be older than 40. Their fossil bones sometimes showed injuries such as broken arms. This may be due to the way they hunted. Scientists think Neanderthals would often directly face animals, jabbing them with spears, rather than keeping their distance and throwing spears or using bows and arrows. This was a risky way of hunting.

The picture below is from an exhibit in the Neanderthal Museum in Croatia. The models are based on over 900 Neanderthal fossil bones found at a site in Croatia. Some of the bones show injuries, mostly to the head and arms.

Decorating themselves

Although life was hard, Neanderthals found time to make decorations to wear. We think they used feathers, shells and animal claws to decorate themselves – either to look more attractive or for special occasions.

In a cave in northern Italy, scientists have found the remains of the wings of birds, such as vultures, eagles, falcons and wood pigeons. On the wings are cut marks which suggest Neanderthals may have taken off the larger feathers. The feathers may have been used to decorate themselves. Feathers have been found mixed with Neanderthal bones.

In central France, body ornaments made by Neanderthals dating from about 44 thousand years ago have been found. They are shown in the picture. There are polished stones and eagle claws with holes made in them. These may have been used for necklaces, pendants or bracelets.

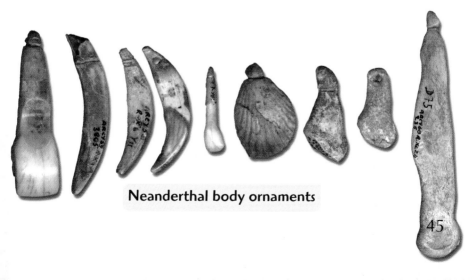

Neanderthal body ornaments

The shells shown in the picture below were found in a cave in Spain. They date from between 115 thousand and 120 thousand years ago. Neanderthals have made holes in them. The shells were painted with colours made from plants and minerals.

This is how Neanderthals may have decorated themselves with feathers and paints made from plants and minerals.

Digging for Neanderthal remains in Spain – The strings in the photo form a grid which shows where fossils and tools were found. Notes are written to give further details of the finds.

What happened to Neanderthals?

Around 40 thousand years ago, Neanderthals died out – they became extinct. How did this happen? Nobody really knows. A number of reasons have been given.

Climate change and food. At this time, we know there were sudden changes in the climate and some of the large animals that Neanderthals hunted died out, and so did some plants. Neanderthals may not have been able to find enough food.

Contact with *Homo sapiens*. As the climate changed, *Homo sapiens* were moving out of Africa and into Europe. *Homo sapiens* hunted the same animals and collected the same plants as Neanderthals, so Neanderthals would have had to compete with them for food and other resources.

Neanderthals live on

Recently, scientists made an amazing discovery. They found that Neanderthals didn't die out completely because they live on as part of the **DNA** of most people today. How do we know this? We know because scientists are now able to examine DNA from fossil bones.

DNA contains the genes we inherit from our ancestors. Genes are the instructions for making our bodies and our brains. DNA can tell us that a fossil hominin was male or female and maybe even the colour of their eyes, skin and hair.

scraping a Neanderthal bone to look for DNA

It can also tell us if there had been any **interbreeding** between different types of hominins. By comparing the DNA of Neanderthals and modern humans, we can tell that most of us have some Neanderthal genes.

When *Homo sapiens* moved into Europe about 45 thousand years ago, they came into contact with Neanderthals. *Homo sapiens* and Neanderthals sometimes interbred (had children together). This is how Neanderthal genes have been passed down to us.

Today there are about seven billion people in the world. Most of us have some Neanderthal genes in our DNA. We usually have between 1% and 2% Neanderthal genes.

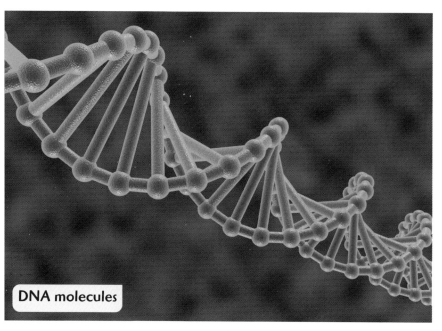

DNA molecules

Neanderthals: in brief

The earliest Neanderthal fossils are dated to 430 thousand years ago. They lived in Europe and Asia. They were well-built with powerful muscles but in many ways they were like us. They were skilful hunters and ate large amounts of meat. They decorated themselves with paint and jewellery made from shells, feathers and animal claws.

Around 40 thousand years ago they died out. However, for several thousand years they interbred with *Homo sapiens* and today most of us have some Neanderthal genes in our DNA.

Timeline

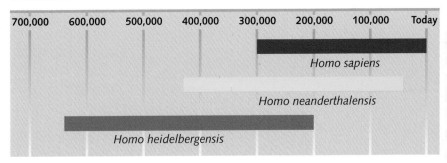

| 700,000 | 600,000 | 500,000 | 400,000 | 300,000 | 200,000 | 100,000 | Today |

Homo sapiens

Homo neanderthalensis

Homo heidelbergensis

50

7 Denisovans (den-i-so-vans)

In 2010, scientists studied part of a small fossil finger bone found in a cave in Siberia in Russia. They could tell from studying the DNA that it belonged to a young girl. They thought she came from a group of hominins which they called *Denisovans* after the name of the cave – Denisova Cave.

DNA taken from the finger bone showed that the *Denisovans* were similar in some ways to both *Homo sapiens* and Neanderthals, but different in other ways.

Although we know about the genes of the *Denisovans*, we don't know much about their way of life or what they looked like. But we know they had large jaws, and they were probably strong and heavily built and probably more like Neanderthals than *Homo sapiens*.

Denisova Cave in Siberia, Russia

The oldest known *Denisovan* fossil is about 285 thousand years old. However, their DNA suggests *Denisovans* probably evolved at least 450 thousand years ago and died out around 40 thousand years ago, about the same time as Neanderthals. Some scientists think that, like Neanderthals, they may have evolved from *Homo heidelbergensis*.

Some *Denisovans* interbred with both Neanderthals and *Homo sapiens*. A toe bone belonging to another girl who died over 50 thousand years ago was found in Denisova Cave. Her genes show that her mother was a Neanderthal and her father was a *Denisovan*. Scientists called her *Denny*.

an artist's view of what Denny may have looked like

In 2019, we heard some exciting news. Part of a jawbone found a few years earlier was shown by scientists to be from a *Denisovan*. The jawbone remains had been found in a cave in Gansu Province, China, over 2000 km southeast of Denisova Cave.

Gansu Province

Like the area around Denisova Cave, this is a moutainous area with low oxygen levels which can make it difficult to breathe. However, *Denisovan* DNA contains a gene which helps people breathe when oxygen is low.

This gene is found in many people who live in the area today. It probably comes from the interbreeding of early *Homo sapiens* with *Denisovans* living in mountainous areas.

Small amounts of *Denisovan* DNA are found today in many people in Asia and much larger amounts (up to about 5%) in **indigenous peoples** in Australia, the Philippines and Papua New Guinea.

Denisovans, Neanderthals and *Homo sapiens* met, mixed and had children together. This shows that interbreeding was a key part of recent human evolution.

Children from Gansu Province probably still have some *Denisovan* genes.

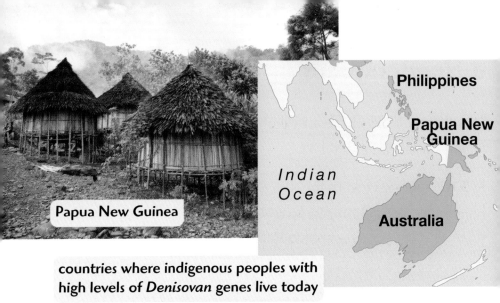

countries where indigenous peoples with high levels of *Denisovan* genes live today

Denisovans: **in brief**

The DNA of *Denisovans* shows they were similar in some ways to both Neanderthals and *Homo sapiens* but different in other ways. Some *Denisovans* interbred with both Neanderthals and *Homo sapiens*. Today, *Denisovans* genes are found in the DNA of groups of people in parts of Asia and Australasia.

Timeline

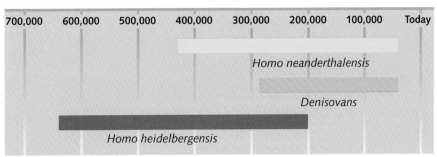

54

8 *Homo sapiens* (sap-ee-ens) – **wise human**

This chapter looks at the arrival of us. We are *Homo sapiens* which means "wise humans".

In 2017, scientists told us that hominin fossils found in Morocco, north Africa, were the oldest *Homo sapiens* fossils ever found. They were about 300 thousand years old, maybe even older.

unearthing human bones in Morocco

What was found? First the fossil bones of five people – skulls, teeth, and arm and leg bones which were similar in some ways to those of today's humans.

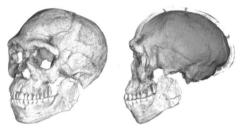

front and side view of a reconstruction of a 300-thousand-year-old *Homo sapiens* skull from Morocco

Along with the human fossils were a large number of well-made stone tools, which were very like stone tools found in eastern and southern Africa.

Stone tools found in Morocco – Some of them may have been used for spear heads. No hand axes were found.

55

At the time of the first *Homo sapiens*, part of today's Sahara Desert in north Africa was warm and wet with widespread grasslands, clumps of trees, rivers and giant lakes.

Large amounts of animal bones have been found there, along with the stone tools – fossils of gazelles, some wildebeest, zebras and buffaloes, hares, porcupines, tortoises, snakes, ostrich eggs and freshwater shellfish.

The bones often had cut marks, some were charred and burnt and found with lumps of **charcoal**. This shows the meat was cooked by these early *Homo sapiens*.

Although the Moroccan fossils are the oldest *Homo sapiens* bones found so far, other *Homo sapiens* bones have been found in South Africa dated from about 260 thousand years ago and in Ethiopia dated from about 195 thousand years ago.

The river of human evolution

Many of today's scientists think that *Homo sapiens* came from the whole of the African continent. They think there was no single place of arrival, that we didn't come from a single group and there was no straight line of evolution.

There were lots of early *Homo sapiens* groups in Africa. They may have had children together and so their genes would have been shared. They also shared their skills and ideas. Stone tools were often similar across many parts of Africa as modern humans evolved.

There is some evidence to show that *Homo sapiens* evolved from *Homo heidelbergensis*. But many scientists now believe that we evolved from several groups of hominins that lived across Africa.

At times, our evolution was like a river with different streams flowing into it, sometimes separating from it and sometimes rejoining the main river.

In the same way, different groups of hominins came together and interbred, some died out, some passed their genes on to other groups, some rejoined groups they had left, as *Homo sapiens* gradually evolved.

But today is different. Now we have evolved into one type of hominin, *Homo sapiens* – us.

some of the places in Africa where early *Homo sapiens* fossils have been found

Homo sapiens: **in brief**

In 2017, the earliest *Homo sapiens* fossils were found in Morocco, north Africa. They were about 300 thousand years old, maybe even older. Large amounts of stone tools and animal bones were found with the human fossils. Also found were charred animal bones and lumps of charcoal which indicated that animal meat was cooked.

Timeline

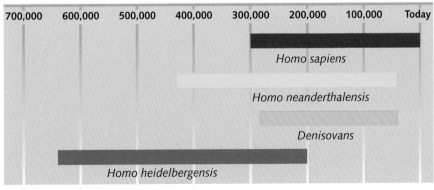

9 Becoming human – art and music

How are we different from other animals? What makes us human? We know there are some things that are special to humans today such as the pictures we paint and the music we play. But we are not sure how long ago we started to paint and play music, to decorate ourselves with jewellery and to sing and dance.

Blombos Cave

One of the oldest pieces of art we know about made by *Homo sapiens* was found in Blombos Cave in South Africa. It is a pattern carved on a piece of soft stone called red ochre and dated to about 75 thousand years ago. Ochre was ground up by *Homo sapiens* to make red, yellow or brown paint.

red ochre with a carved pattern found in Blombos Cave

Blombos Cave has been called a "red ochre paint factory" because tool kits have been found there for mixing red ochre with crushed bone, fat, charcoal and a mineral rock called quartz to make paint.

The paint may have been used for face and body painting, and to paint shells, stones, animal skins or pictures on cave walls.

a shell bowl used to mix paint, found in Blombos Cave and dated to about 100 thousand years ago

Ochre is still used for decoration today, as shown by this photograph of a Samburu warrior in Kenya.

Jewellery and self-decoration

Shell beads were probably some of the first kinds of jewellery made by *Homo sapiens*. The picture below shows shell beads found in Blombos Cave in South Africa and dated to around 100 thousand years ago.

The beads were found in groups of similar size and colours. This probably means that each group of beads was a separate necklace or bracelet. Shell beads believed to be 70 thousand to at least 110 thousand years old have also been found in Algeria, Morocco and the eastern Mediterranean region.

shell beads found in Blombos Cave

Paintings

One of the oldest **figurative paintings** – a painting of a figure such as an animal or person – was found in a cave in Borneo, an island in south-east Asia. The painting shows wild cattle and is at least 40 thousand years old. In a nearby cave, there are hand stencils about 50 thousand years old, made by blowing mouthfuls of paint over a hand held against the rock. Ancient hand stencils are found in caves across the world.

hand stencils in Borneo

Another example of an early figurative cave painting was discovered in Indonesia in southeast Asia in 2017. It shows small stick-like animals, and humans hunting buffaloes and other animals. It is about 44 thousand years old.

the cave painting found in Indonesia

a cave painting in India

In central India, there are over 500 caves with paintings up to 30 thousand years old. They often show hunting scenes with bows and arrows and spears, and animals such as bison, tigers, elephants, antelopes and rhinoceroses. Also pictured are human figures dancing and celebrating.

In north-western Australia there are thousands of rock art paintings – paintings on rocks rather than in caves. They were done by Indigenous Australians. Some may be 40 thousand years old or even older.

rock painting of a kangaroo in northern Australia

63

Some of the oldest cave art from Europe was found in Chauvet Cave in southeastern France. It may be around 30 thousand years old. The picture shows horses and a rhinoceros. The cave wall was scraped clean before the painting was made with charcoal. Also painted in the cave are lions, bears, stags and mammoths.

a painting from Chauvet Cave

Carving

Some of the earliest carved figures have been found in caves in southern Germany, all carved from the tusks of woolly mammoths. Two of these carvings are shown in the following pictures.

Known today as *lion man*, this figure is 30 centimetres tall with what looks like the head of a lion and the body of a human. It is about 38 thousand years old.

This carving of a wild horse is about 40 thousand years old.

Music

We don't really know when music was invented by
modern humans. It probably began with singing and dancing
and handclapping. The first musical instruments may have been
drums and rattles but since they were made of wood, animal
skins or plants, they have rotted away so we have no evidence
of them.

The earliest musical instruments that have been found are flutes.
The picture shows a flute made from a vulture's wing bone,
found in Germany and dated to about 40 thousand years ago.
It has four holes and a V-shaped mouthpiece. Several other
flutes made from mammoth tusks, dating from about
35 thousand years ago, have also been found in Germany.

flute made from a vulture's wing bone

Becoming human

What does art and music say about us as human beings? Could these examples of art and music mean that early *Homo sapiens* have become human beings as we know ourselves today? Some scientists would answer "Yes".

But earlier hominins, such as Neanderthals, also made body ornaments from shells, stones and feathers. There is evidence that they used paint to decorate themselves as well. So where does being a modern human like us begin?

Homo sapiens have imagination and creativity. This can be seen in ancient painting, carving, jewellery and musical instruments. Painting means that these early humans recalled things, saw them in their mind, then made them into pictures.

Young people today painting and making music, just like their ancestors thousands of years ago.

Music means they probably created tunes and rhythms and they sang and danced.

Homo sapiens prepared and planned ahead. We know this because they prepared for art with tool kits for making paint and they sometimes scraped cave walls before painting them. Does imagination and making art and music show they had become like today's humans?

Art and music: **in brief**

The early art and music created by early *Homo sapiens* can be seen as evidence that they were becoming more like us. They indicate human imagination and creativity. The first indications of art date from over 100 thousand years ago. The earliest figurative paintings date from at least 44 thousand years ago.

10 Out of Africa

Homo sapiens came from Africa. We now live all over the world. When did we move out of Africa? How did we find our way around the world? Fossils and stone tools can give us clues.

The oldest *Homo sapiens* fossil outside of Africa that we know about was found in Apidima Cave in Greece. It is the back of a skull at least 210 thousand years old.

Apidima Cave today –
The sea level was much lower
210 thousand years ago.

the side and back view
of the skull found in
Apidima Cave

Routes out of Africa

The following map shows two of the routes that *Homo sapiens* may have taken out of Africa and into Asia. There were probably many migrations out of Africa, and some back into Africa too.

Homo sapiens reached Australia around 65 thousand years ago or perhaps even earlier. Thousands of stone tools have been found in northern Australia that are at least 65 thousand years old. Sea levels then were much lower than they are today. People walked over land for some of their journeys, but they would have needed boats to get to places like New Guinea and Australia.

This map shows possible routes out of Africa and across Asia.

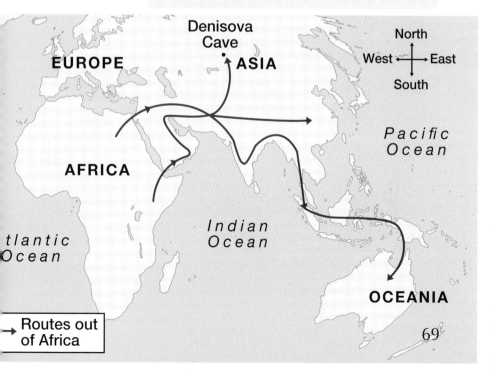

Homo sapiens walked into Europe about 45 thousand years ago. We think people travelled north from Africa and went along the southern coast of Europe to Italy, France and Spain, as shown by Route 1 on the map below. Some people may have moved from Africa to Asia and then travelled west into Europe, as shown by Route 2 on the map.

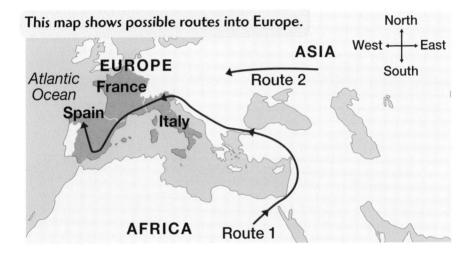

This map shows possible routes into Europe.

Moving into North and South America

Travelling to North and South America was one of the last big journeys made by *Homo sapiens*. The map opposite shows two possible routes.

The first people to arrive in the Americas probably came by land. Sea levels were much lower than they are today because big **ice sheets** had locked up a lot of water. This gave a **land bridge** between Siberia in north-eastern Asia and North America.

In 2021, scientists found 60 human footprints made in the muddy shores of a shallow lake in the south-western United States. They were probably made between 21 and 23 thousand years ago. Today they are hardened and preserved under white sand.

A second route to the Americas was probably by sea. Some people may have travelled in boats as far south as Monte Verde near the bottom of South America. Fireplaces, charcoal and burnt animal bones found in Monte Verde showed that people may have lived there more than 15 thousand years ago.

This map shows possible routes into North and South America.

This picture below shows people carrying birds and fish back to the camp. Other people are cutting up and cooking a large deer. It is an artist's view, based on things found in an excavation in Alaska that are thought to be 14 thousand years old.

Why travel out of Africa?

For about 95% of our existence as human beings, we lived as hunter-gatherers. We depended on gathering fruit, berries, leaves, nuts and roots, and hunting animals for food.

Big changes in temperature and rainfall can affect plant life and the animals that feed on the plants. If the rainfall became far less, then the grasslands might become deserts and many plants would die out.

The animals that feed on them would either die or move to places with more rainfall. Hunter-gatherer people are also likely to move as they need plant food and animals to eat.

Being able to travel to another place may also depend on the weather. Very low temperatures can lead to the land being covered with ice. A lot of water is frozen. This can lead to low sea levels which could have made it easier to travel. Examples of this are the land bridge to North America and the shorter distances between the islands leading to Australia.

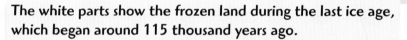

The white parts show the frozen land during the last ice age, which began around 115 thousand years ago.

11 The story of us continues

More fossils, more stone tools and more cave paintings are found every year. The story of human evolution is constantly developing. We now have new ways to learn more about things we find, such as examining DNA.

The following example shows some gum taken from a birch tree and used as chewing gum. It was found in Denmark and it was thought to be 5700 years old. Using just this small piece of gum, scientists were able to examine the DNA of the person who had been chewing it.

The DNA could tell them that the person who had been chewing it was a young female with black hair, blue eyes and dark skin.

She also left bits of her latest meal in the gum – duck and hazelnuts.

the gum which the girl had been chewing

an artist's view of what the girl might have looked like, based on her DNA

Over a hundred years ago, in 1903, a skeleton was found in Cheddar Caves in Somerset, south-west England. It is thought to be about ten thousand years old and scientists called it Cheddar Man.

It was only recently, in 2018, that new technology was used to examine Cheddar Man's DNA and find out what he probably looked like. Cheddar Man's genes indicated that he had dark skin, blue eyes and black hair. Artists made a model of how we think he looked.

There will be many exciting things discovered as time goes on. You can keep up with new finds if you search online for "human evolution" and the current year. These discoveries mean we are continuing to understand the story of us.

Cheddar Man

Glossary

ancestors people or creatures from which a person or a creature is descended; for example, for humans our grandparents and, a long way further back, ape-like creatures

charcoal burnt wood

DNA molecules in every cell of living things which contain genes instructing the organism how to function, how to grow and how to look; for example, in humans how tall to grow, how our eyes work and what colour our hair is

excavations (also known as digs) when an area is dug up and studied to find evidence of the past

figurative paintings paintings of a figure such as a person or an animal

fossils the remains of once-living things which have turned to stone

hominins creatures which have one or more human-like features that are not found in apes

ice sheets thick layers of ice covering a large area of land for a long period of time

indigenous peoples people who first lived in an area

interbreeding different types of hominins having children together

land bridge a strip of land which connects two landmasses (large areas of land)

pyrite also known as iron pyrite, a mineral which makes sparks when hit by another piece of pyrite, a piece of flint or iron

Index

Human evolution timelines

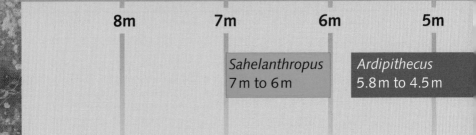

	8m	7m	6m	5m
		Sahelanthropus 7m to 6m	Ardipithecus 5.8m to 4.5m	

800,000	700,000	600,000	500,000	400,
		Homo heidelbergensis 640,000 to 200,000		

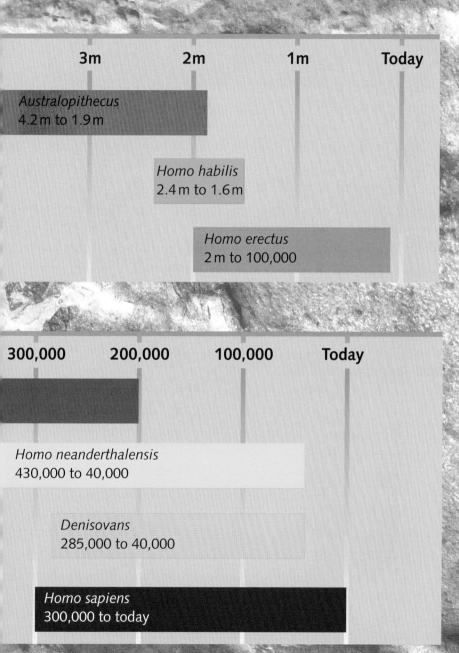

Ideas for reading

Written by Gill Matthews
Primary Literacy Consultant

Reading objectives:

- summarise the main ideas drawn from more than one paragraph, identifying key details that support the main ideas
- retrieve, record and present information from non-fiction
- explain and discuss their understanding of what they have read, including through formal presentations and debates, maintaining a focus on the topic and using notes where necessary

Spoken language objectives:

- ask relevant questions to extend their understanding and knowledge
- maintain attention and participate actively in collaborative conversations, staying on topic and initiating and responding to comments
- participate in discussions, presentations, performances, role play, improvisations and debates

Curriculum links: History – Changes in Britain from the Stone Age to the Iron Age; Science – Evolution and inheritance

Interest words: imagination, creativity, prepared, planned

Build a context for reading

- Ask children to explore the cover of the book. Discuss their predictions about the content of the book.
- Ask what they know about how humans have developed.
- Ask what organisational features they think the book might have, for example, a contents page, index and glossary.
- Ask them to turn to the contents page and to find and read the introduction. Discuss their understanding of what the book is about, encouraging children to ask questions in order to clarify their understanding.

Understand and apply reading strategies

- Read Chapter 1 aloud, asking children to note down key information. Support children in summarising the information given in this chapter.